Table of Content

That seems to be a lot of content that I want to convey to you here, right? Basically, drifting is not so difficult. Are you up for it? Then let's start right now!

Simon Tillisch - Who Am I?

My name is Simon Tillisch and I am enthusiastic about vehicle technology, speed and adrenaline. Even in my childhood days I could barely wait to move faster than simply walking. At 18, the driving license and the car were added - absolute chaos for my fellow men! I love driving and accordingly, I have informed myself about technical connections, you could say it is a kind of passion for me. This somehow went so far that I could start to recognize different car models solely by their sounds. Which was very impressive to my friends. With the purchase of my first BMW also the sporty driving was sealed. However, there was still something I had a lot of respect for. Just when it had rained or even snow fell, I in the beginning was quite unsure what my vehicle rear there actually did. Nevertheless, I could not slow down and the topic of drifting became more and more interesting to me. Since September 2014, however, I have decided to approach the topic a lot more professionally. I got a second vehicle and participated in events. The journey from the absolute newbie to the more experienced participant has not always been easy. It took a lot of time and material. With this workshop, I would like to tell you, dear reader, all the basics you need for drifting. It took me several months to gather such information. In my circle of acquaintances, there are many people who are interested in drifting, want to test it, or even want to participate in events themselves. So it would be practical if all the information is made available compact and digital form, right?

That´s me, Simon Tillisch, with our Syron-Team vehicle at the Tuning World Bodensee 2017, organized by Alex Gräff.

Thanks a lot at this place !

Basic Knowledge

Drifting

The word "drift" is used when something moves without a specific destination, such as a raft would do. In fact, it is also called "drift off". But what does this have to do with motorsport, which is all about vehicle control? There drifting is used in different sectors in order to drive with a higher speed in the corners, for example during a rally. In essence, the driver tries to move his vehicle into a targeted oversteering while maintaining control and speed. Meanwhile, this is regarded as a globally recognized sport in which angle, elegance and speed account for points that are given by a jury.

In this context, I would like to quote a man who, through his driving skills, has established himself among the car enthusiasts and has also won numerous prizes. Nowadays he is considered a racing legend. He said the following about drifting:

"Good drivers have the flies on their side windows."
and
"Drifting is the art of keeping an unstable state stable."

This is nothing short of Walter Röhrl.

Drivetrain

A drivetrain is the way in which the vehicle converts its power to the ground. There are front-wheel drive vehicles whose front wheels are driven, rear-wheel drive vehicles whose rear wheels are driven, and four-wheel drive vehicles, in which all four wheels in the drivetrain maintain tension and move the vehicle forward. The possibility to drift is mainly offered with rear-wheel vehicles, which are therefore mainly used in drifting. I would advise you to do the same. In the case of all-wheel drive vehicles, it is also possible, but only with enough power surplus. Front-driven vehicles are rather unsuitable for drifting, but there are exceptions. The latter two will be explained in the "Grip" section.

Vehicle Selection

The car selection is sometimes one of the most important topics, because here lies your base with which you then proceed. We already know that rear-wheel-driven vehicles are best suited for this purpose. But what else is important? The weight distribution! This starts with the engine placement in the vehicle. We need as little weight as possible on the rear axis, so we are looking for a vehicle whose engine is installed in the front. There are also possibilities of middle and rear engines where the engine is positioned directly behind the driver, or just installed in the rear, similar to a VW Beetle. Just recently, I read a report in which someone said that a rear engine would be best suited for a beginner because of the weight on the rear axis. When I read this suddenly my leg fell off. Well. So in the beginning please take a vehicle with a front engine. Otherwise the additional weight in the rear makes it extremely difficult to control a car specifically whilst drifting. Thus, the boundary area and the clearance are also very small. Since we are already on the topic of weight: The car should not be too heavy. So not exactly a bulldozer of a car. Keep it compact, but not too compact. With a short wheelbase it is like using a kart, which again limits the border area. The best choice is a middle-class vehicle. In addition I would look for a somewhat older car. Not only because of the purchase costs, but also because of the spare parts you might need. It is also always an idea of the mechanical functioning of the vehicle, without the whole electronics of the cars nowadays. In terms of engine technology, it is not so important to have an excessive amount of performance. Some displacement and thus torque is decisive. This means that the wheels get more power than they get on the road with their adhesive force. I decided on my first drift car to have a petrol engine, because a gasoline engine allows me to drive at high speeds and, if necessary, to pull off a drift sometimes through the speed range. So what is important? I summarize:

• Front engine
• Rear drive
• Lightweight
• a bit older
• Keep compact
• Petrol engine
• Engine with "some displacement"

With these criteria, I came across my BMW e36 328i, which still faithfully accompanies me today in the motorsport.

Differential

Perhaps the term "differential" is already known to you, but I would like to briefly discuss the function and explain the connection to drifting. The differential is fastened underneath the vehicle between the drive shafts and the cardan shaft and is an integral part of your drivetrain, which provides for the propulsion. The differential has the function of equalizing different fast turns of the wheels. Imagine you're driving to a place of your choice. On the way you have different curves that you are driving. When cornering, the following happens: The inner edge of the curve is shorter than the outer edge of the curve, so the interior is smaller than the outer wheel. Consequently, the interior must also rotate less than the exterior. This is compensated by a mechanical gear system in the differential in order to achieve a higher driving comfort and to "park smoothly" or to drive curves. In sporty driving, however, this is rather negative, because when the cornering is smooth, the vehicle tends toward the outside edge of the curve and thus automatically weighs more on the outside of the curve. This, combined with fast driving, leads to the inner wheel spinning, while the other preserves its liability and does not. Exceptions are, of course, journeys on snow or ice, sometimes even on a wet road, since here both wheels can develop little adhesion and thus the possibility exists that both wheels rotate simultaneously. On a dry road drifting like this is more like a pitiful attempt. The so-called "limited slip differential" creates a remedy here. More on this in the chapter "Differential Modifications".

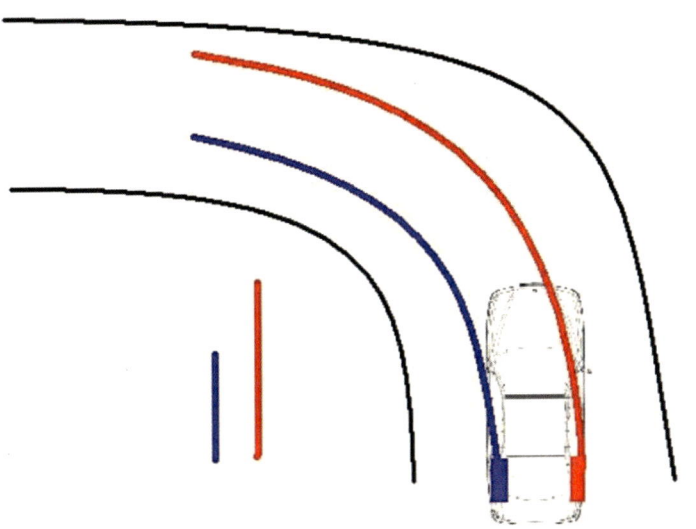

Here's an example for you. As you can see, the **right** and the **left** tire have different distances. So the right tire needs to turn more often as the left one.

Tires

As you have already guessed, tires are an elementary part of the sport of drifting - without a question. Are there any differences? Sure they exist! A new tire is much different from an old, hardened tire. Even the fact that new tires have a lot more profile and so you can "run through" several rounds one after another without changing the wheel sounds damn good, right? But honestly, who already has the fortune to put in a dozen new tires every day for heating in the garage? Most professional drivers are sponsored by tire manufacturers. In the beginning, however, there is usually no other option but to access old used tires. But I do not think that is so bad. Many workshops and service stations have a lot of used tires, which they would have to dispose cost-intensive. Maybe you can talk to them and buy them off for a bargain. Ask friends or acquaintances if they have an old wheel set that fits your car. In this way I have accumulated many sets of wheels.

Tip: You want to drift without getting on the nerves of your own environment? Take winter tires, these squeak at a lower frequency and are not that loud.

I know wide tires with big rims look really cool! However, you should keep in the back of your mind that the tires wide bearing surface must have a corresponding performance in order to overcome this adhesion and to make the tires spin. Therefore, you should definitely start rear narrow tires with a small inch size, in order to get a feeling for drifting. For example, I am currently driving on my BMW e36 328i the tire width 185 to 205 with the size of 15 inches. At the front of the steering wheel, you can use a wider tire of good quality because it keeps you on track. We finally want to drift and not run through the area out of control.

Adhesive Force

The issue of adhesive force is essential when drifting. But what is it exactly? Adhesive force is the result of sufficient adhesion friction. This is a force that prevents the moving body from touching. This occurs, for example, by a physically acting force or by the entanglement of unevenness in the surface. Simply put: If you drive your vehicle on asphalt, the vehicle weight pushes you to the ground your profile in the asphalt. These two components combine to give you adhesion, which must be overcome when drifting.

Even with all-wheel drive vehicles you can drift, but as mentioned above, there must be sufficient power, so that all four wheels can spin at the same time and lose their adhesion. In addition, all-wheel drifts are rather a sideways movement in which one has to turn into the curve, not as usual obliquely forward with counter-steering. Because if you turn here, you quickly land in the road ditch. Finally, the front wheels are also driving, which then pull the vehicle outwards. "Drifting" with front-wheel drive vehicles also works under special conditions. Here, "drifting" is also rather a controlled blocking of the rear wheels with the handbrake, by which one slides laterally. This works very well if the grip of the rear wheels is largely eliminated, for example by bad tires, wet or snow-covered road or by clamping something under its blocked tires, for example a wooden board. Drifting for me is however rather a controlled gas to move the vehicle to the eruption and if necessary accelerate in the drift.

Tip: The adhesion deficit of a wet or snow-covered road can also be used greatly in combination with rear-wheel drive and open serial differential. The wheels develop so little ground adhesion that both spin and the differential does not split the force on the wheel with less resistance. Thus, it is possible to drift with a serial vehicle.

Theory - Vehicle Preparation

Differential Modifications

Many automotive manufacturers offer differentials in their assortment with 25%, sometimes even 45% blocking. This means that when the vehicle is traversing the wheel that is loaded with less weight or less spinning will have at least 25% or 45% of the power and thus propulsion is ensured. There are many automobile manufacturers who block the locking differentials in their sporty models, as they bring the power to the road better. What different types of locks there are and which are worthwhile, I'll tell you soon. If you are a drifter you can also make it easier by welding your existing differential and thus bridging the mechanical aspect of compensation. Here, a 100% barrier effect similar to a rigid axis is obtained and thus a constant, simultaneous acceleration of both wheels. By the way, this is the variant with which I currently drift and in my opinion from the cost factor seen absolutely worthwhile. Thanks to the even distribution of power on both wheels, a drift can be simply initiated and, with some practice, also simply controlled.

(This picture was taken to a public forum for demonstration)

This is how a welded differential looks. The drive shaft gears on the right and left were welded to the upper and lower compensating wheels. In the middle there is a metal plate to ensure the stability. Now one has a complete rigid axle.

Locked Differentials

Do you want to drift with your daily vehicle and use a locked differential? Then the welded differential is nothing for you. But what are the possibilities? On the one hand there is the "Torsen differential". This differential acts "torque-sensing". Here, however, we have the problem that this type of differential will only shift the drive torque between the driven wheels, rather than the axis being locked as we need it for our purposes. Thus this type is rather unsuitable. On the other hand there is the "Viscodifferential". This lock acts "speed-sensing" and blocks from a certain rotational speed difference of the driven wheels. As the name already indicates, this barrier type works by the fact that a special oil in the barrier body changes its viscosity and restricts the installed lamella pack in its movement. Unfortunately, this type of lock is very sluggish and therefore unsuitable for our purposes. We need the lock immediately on call. This works best with the proven "Lamellar Lock". Why proven? The Lamellar lock has been used in motorsports since the 1950s. This lock contains special friction lamella which are pressed against one another via pressure plates. The degree of blocking is variably adjustable by various factors. In addition, a pretension can be set by means of socalled "plate springs" so that the lamellas are permanently pressed onto one another. This results in a constant barrier effect which is also present without load or even in the vehicle's standing. My recommendation clearly is using the Lamellar lock! Lamellar locks can easily be found on the Internet.

Weight Reduction

The weight reduction is, in my opinion, a very fun topic. It says nothing more than "throw everything from your car, which you do not need to drift". We finally know that the weight on the rear axis pushes the wheels to the ground and thus more unwanted adhesion arises.

Tip: You should start removing loose items such as backpacks, pawns, or other items. These can also become a safety risk with rapid driving.

Spare wheel? We have enough in the garage. Back seat? At the back, no one drives, so off! Foot mats? Not with us. Comfort means weight.

This is how my vehicle looks after my "fitness program".

Interior

Also of importance is the interior, I do not mean the leather equipment, but a motorsports-suitable equipment with security aspect. Good seats with side rails and proper seat belts are very important. Many drifters change from the normal cable tension brake to a hydraulic handbrake, since it engages the rear disc brakes via a separate brake circuit and has a stronger braking force than the standard drum brake. In addition, there is no chance that the cable will break, or you will destroy your drum brake. Here I will show you a sample picture.

Electronic Assistants

With the electronic assistants, I of course mean, the assistance systems, which are built for safety reasons in everyday road traffic. These, however, interfere with drifting. Particularly disturbing is the traction control, which ensures that the gas intake is screwed back when the wheels are screwed back in order to prevent that. Also the ABS, which was designed to trigger the brake during dangling brakes, and thus to prevent the tires from completely blocking, should be switched off. I put them both on a switch, so I can turn it off completely with one button.

Tire Pressure

Yes, we already had the category of tires, but there is also one or another tip which can help you to drift. You already know that you should take narrow tires. But do you know how much air pressure you should fill it with? This is also part of the preparations. What happens when you pump a lot of pressure into a tire? On the one hand, it becomes harder and on the other hand the profile center slightly curves outwards. Thus we can reduce the bearing surface of the tire again and it is easier to get it to spin. However, you should always remember that the air in the tire is heated by the drifting process just as much as the tire itself and the air expands. Start with a little less pressure. Your tires also last a bit longer, as if you are already starting with overpressure.

Attention: Please note the maximum pressure of the tire. Not that he still bursts and flies around your ears. I mostly drive to drift the tire pressure 2.7 - 3 bar.

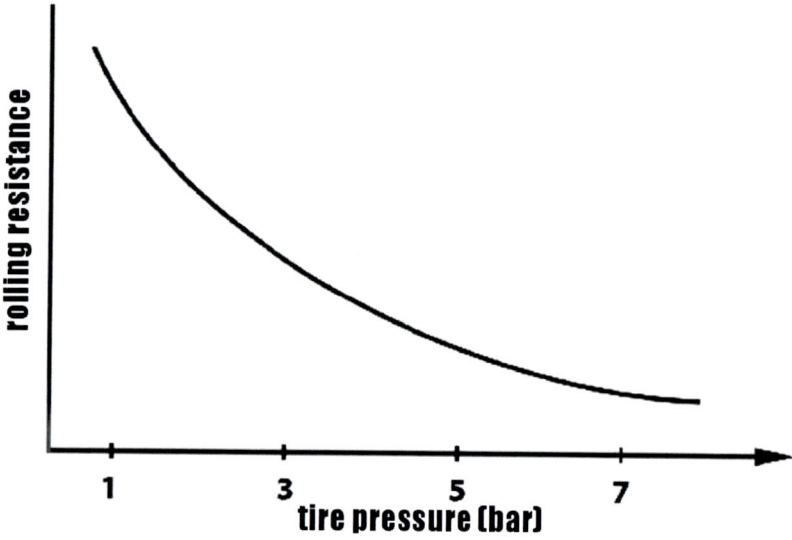

Here is a diagram which symbolizes the rolling resistance in relation to the tire air pressure.

Suspension

In the case of differential, we gained the knowledge that the vehicle tilts to the side when cornering and the weight affects the adhesion of the outer wheels. You can lower the center of gravity of the vehicle by a few centimeters and reduce the lateral inclination with sports suspension, possibly also a lowered spring set. The tighter chassis also leads to less deflection. This is also noticeable and you move as if you were „on rails". A sporty chassis definitely belongs on your To-Do list if you want to move your vehicle accordingly. Here, however, it is important to note a certain degree of hardness. A soft chassis means more traction, a tighter one a better driving position. However, if it is too hard, it is possible that your vehicle starts jumping at ground shafts, since the chassis can not compensate for the unevenness. That this condition is rather bad than right, you can certainly think of. It is quite unfavorable to lose control of your vehicle while drifting, because your rear wheels are suddenly missing the ground contact. In addition, you should always check if your suspension is intact and fully functional. I myself have landed my first vehicle on a tree. Reason: 2 defective shock absorbers.

Driving Stability

The driving stability describes the behavior of your vehicle during bends or side winds. This section is about minimizing the lateral inclination of your vehicle. The first step you have already taken with a tight sports suspension. But there are a few other factors that can influence the driving behavior of your car. You could, for example, consider installing polyurethane sockets on the axis parts of your vehicle. These do not consist like the original sockets made of rubber, but of plastic and do not yield so easily under pressure. So your driving behavior is a little tighter and "crisp". Another possibility would be the change from your stabilizers. The colloquial stabilizer serve as a connection between the right and left suspension components. This has the following background: Imagine you are driving your vehicle with a vehicle side over a floor wave. As a result, the respective vehicle side is spring loaded while the other side is not. Thus, your vehicle will waver and become unstable. The stabilizer counteracts this by, for example, when the right wheel is raised, slightly pulls the left one upwards. Thus, your car experiences less lateral inclination. When drifting you should choose a soft stabilizer at the front for the traction and rear a hard stabilizer for a stiffened rear axle. The strut brace is another point of stability. This connects the opposing spring struts and prevents the position of the domes from changing relative to each other. You run less danger to loose your track and the

driving behavior becomes much better and more direct, especially when cornering.

I also installed a strut brace in my BMW. In the meantime, there are various braces available even without registration.

Steering Angle

Wisefab - This should known by every drifter who has dealt deeper with the technical subject matter. This company offers complete steering angle kits for various vehicles. With a changed steering angle, it is possible to drive a higher drift angle, in extreme conversions even up to 90 °. The disadvantage here is that the complete kits are quite expensive. But we would not be drifters if we were not able to help each other in different situations. There is a cost-effective alternative called spacer. These spacers are nothing else than metal sleeves and serve as spacers on the steering rod. They are attached to the thread that goes into the steering gear. But be careful: If you now have a shorter thread, there is a risk that it will tear under load when drifting. Therefore, you should remove some material from the ball head that you have the full thread available again.

Here you can see that about 3 mm of material has been removed from the left ball head and therefore more threads are available.

And here we see the steering rod Built-in spacer (bronze color).

As you can see, this little thing has a very strong effect on the steering angle. If you drive a converted steering angle for the first time, then please note that your steering movement is going to be a lot sharper. You should get used to this circumstance.

At this point, thank you to Arthur Lelonek for the artwork.

Engine

The engine is subjected to the greatest strain during drifting together with the drive train. Make it as simple as possible: Ensure sufficient cooling. I've seen quite a lot of colleagues whose cars had to die at events with an outside temperature of 40 °. Mine went on cheerfully. This is also due to the fact that I have mounted spacers on the bonnet suspension so that a small gap is created. The function is logical: cool air is drawn from the front. It can flow through the engine compartment, cools the engine there and then flows through the gap across the windshield again outside. In addition to the sufficient coolant you should always take care of enough oil. Due to the high load, oil changes are not uncommon in a drift vehicle within 2000km.

Note: You can also install an ad for your oil temperature. When the oil has reached its operating temperature, it provides its full lubricity. Only then should the engine be fully loaded.

Engine Modifications

"There is nothing like a proper turbocharger," many think. But you should pay attention to a few things. A turbocharger usually delivers the performance in the upper RPM`s, the turbo kick. However, this is difficult to assess at the outset. Especially to keep a turbo vehicle in the drift due to controlled pushes of the gas pedal, since this has a longer response time in contrast to the supercharger. The supercharger is connected directly to the crankshaft of the engine by a belt and therefore reacts immediately. The turbo needs only a certain exhaust gas flow and thus a certain pressure to work properly, this is called the so-called "turbo hole" in the lower speed ranges. In my opinion, a supercharger is also not so wrong, since this works already at low speeds and the performance curve just seen just moved upwards. It does not change the characteristics of the engine except that it provides more power. A good friend told me the best combination he ever drove is a powerful engine with a turbocharger. Due to the displacement, the engine provides enough power to initiate a drift and maintain good performance while the turbocharger's upper speed range unfolds its power. This can be an advantage if you want to accelerate in the drift if you want to pull it into length. How and whether one can upgrade his engine remains left to himself and, above all, to his taste. However, you should then tune it so that the overall characteristic of the motor is correct. This means that, for example, the turbo hole is minimized during a turbo conversion and the power increase is distributed accordingly as far as the speed band is concerned. I myself am of the opinion that a series engine with some displacement without charging is completely enough to collect its first drift experience. You learn how to play with the speed band and to play depending on the gas.

PRACTICE

Important Instructions

Before you go there are a few tips and hints for you:

1. Search a free area with a sufficient run-out area and no other persons or objects nearby. We are here in the border area of a vehicle and just at the beginning you have to learn to assess this. It is advisable to move to a private ground after consultation with the owner. In order to be able to practice perfectly and without disturbing factors, you can visit free training sessions or, as I have done, hire a car park with a few colleagues from time to time.
2. As obstacles, you can take pylons, mark something on the ground with chalk, or use other simple things that do not cause damage.
3. First of all, it is a good idea to practice with snow or wet ground, since you do not have to call up the full power to move the vehicle to the outbreak. It then goes as in slow motion and you have enough time to coordinate your movements.
4. Drifting is usually carried out in the second gear, since this allows a wide range of speed with simultaneous force. Exception is the donut, here you should use the first course.

Attention: Drifting on public roads is not permitted. Since this is a pure transfer of knowledge and information, I assume no liability for damages to persons or objects.

When you're ready, let's get started!

Accelerating

You might think "now why does the acceleration have its own category? Full throttle and ready! The tail will come. " Dear reader, no, it is not like that. Sure, one or the other drift can be initiated with full throttle. But only by the controlled gassing and above all also stepping off the gas(!) During the drift, this becomes controllable. With the throttle you control your drift almost as much as with your steering wheel. This is the only way to change your angle. If you give more gas, the adhesion is reduced more and the vehicle tail pans more. In addition, you can also add length to your drift by correctly using your power. Suppose you are driving on a wet and snowy road. The liability here is a lot lower and it is already a fraction of your accelerator pedal position to force your vehicle into a drift. With too much gas, the whole thing ends quickly with a spin. The right measure is crucial. Less is sometimes more.

"Driving starts for me where I drive the car with the accelerator instead of the steering wheel. Everything else means 'just doing the work'. " - Walter Röhrl

The Donut

The donut is the simplest exercise to familiarize yourself with drifting. Simply place yourself on a free surface and lightly tilt your steering wheel in the direction of your choice. You set the first gear. Now you have to turn the engine up with the clutch pressed and let the clutch "snap" in one stroke, so the gear starts quickly. The tires will spin and you will circle around your own axis. Now you can try to play with the gas and get a feel for the spin of the wheels in connection with the throttle. As a second exercise, you can try to "steer" something out of the rotation and turn the donut into a more drifting drift. To stop, simply interrupt the transmission of the force, ie go from the gas or press the clutch.

Step by step

1. Place on a free surface
2. Lightly turn the steering wheel
3. Set the first gear
4. Press clutch, turn engine up
5. Snap the clutch.

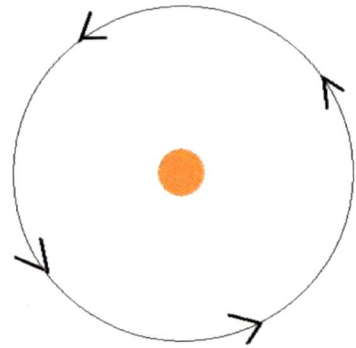

Exercise: After you have twisted a few donuts, you can place a pylone in the middle of your practice area and try to turn around the pylons with a targeted turn. Try to stay as close to the pylons as possible with the inner front wheel. Pick up a pylone and park your car right next to it, so that the pylons and front wheel are at the same height. Now try to turn a donut around the pylons with as little distance to the pylons as possible.

1.Drift with Clutch (easy) (known as "clutch-kick")
When drifting with the clutch, I go as follows: I have the second gear, drive with about 30-40kmh and steer in the direction in which I want to drift. When I am in the corner with my vehicle, I tap the clutch tightly to create a clutch slip, but stay on the throttle, so the engine turns up. I let the clutch snap back directly so that the gear is quickly engaged. As a result, the tires will twist behind and lose their grip. The rear of the vehicle will let itself be carried through the mass to the curvaceous exterior. The vehicle is in drift. Depending on the angle at which the vehicle breaks out, I steer with the steering wheel in the other direction, opposite to the drift.

(Drift to the right -> turn left / drift to the left -> turn right).

Now I can hold the drift with focused throttle and counter-steering. To stop, simply interrupt the transmission of the force, ie go from the gas or press the clutch.

Step by step:

1. Speed 30-40 km / h, second gear engaged
2. Deflecting
3. Press the clutch, turn the engine up
4. Snap the clutch
5. Deflecting the drift with the targeted gas values

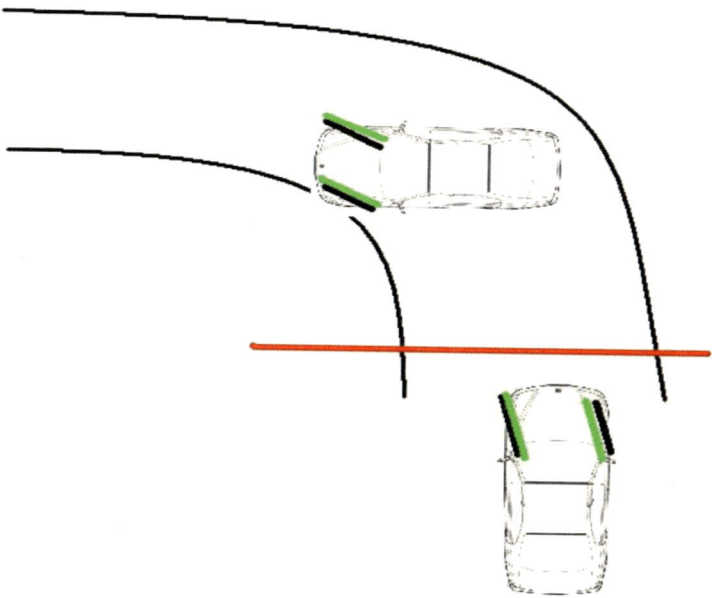

At the **red line** I let the clutch come up, let the vehicle break out and then steer with the steering wheel opposite to the curve.
The **green**-**black** bars show the steering direction.

 Create a square of pylons with enough space. If you are now around the square you can always drive from corner to corner and try to initiate a drift with your clutch, always around the respective corner. On the right you see a view of the exercise. The orange points mark the pylons. Now you can drive around your raised square and try to drift at every corner by letting the clutch come up. Note, however, that you have enough space between the pylons.

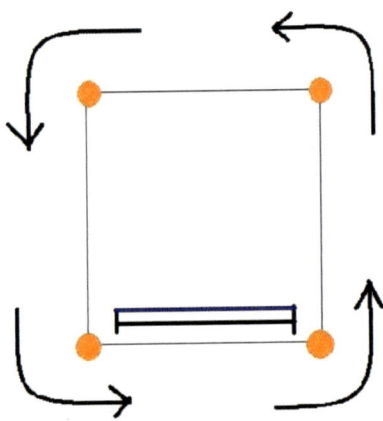

2. Drift with the Handbrake (easy)

Drifting with the handbrake is also a well-known and simple way of initiating a drift. For this I drive with my vehicle to the place where I want to drift (in 2nd gear). At the entrance to the corner I turn back in the direction I want to drift. At the same time, I press the clutch and pull the handbrake so far that the rear wheels block. The vehicle tail will break out. By still pushing the clutch, I can turn the engine up with the gas. Then I release the handbrake completely and let the clutch snap. Now I turn the rear wheels through and I can also keep the vehicle in drift by means of targeted gas jets and counter-steering. To stop simply interrupt the force transmission, so go from the gas or press clutch.

Note: Carefully separate the handbrake and clutch from each other. I pulled the handbrake during my first attempt while I had not pressed the clutch. Result: The power of the engine has destroyed my handbrake.

Step by step:

1st speed ~ 40 km / h, second gear engaged
2. Press the clutch, then pull and brake the hand brake
3. The vehicle starts to slip behind
4. Loosen the handbrake
5. Press the throttle and snap the clutch.
6. Deflecting the drift by means of targeted gasses.

Exercise:

1. As a first step, you can try a handbrake turn to get a feel for it. Drive at 20-40 km / h and pull the handbrake while pressing the clutch. Always hit the steering fully and try to turn your vehicle 180 ° so that you are standing in the opposite direction.

 2. Build a small curve of pylons or paint on the asphalt with chalk. Move to this curve and try to slip through the curve with the hand brake applied. You can also use the Parkour shown in Exercise 1 (Drifting with the clutch).

3. Drifting by Using the Vehicle weight (medium)

I use the mass of the vehicle when drifting by rocking. I drive straight on a curve. Before I reach the curve, however, I steer my vehicle like a slalom on a straight line, one or two times. Let me give you an example. I would like to drift a curve to the left. In a straight line I turn slightly to the left, so I move towards the edge of my lane. Then I quickly turn right towards the right edge of my lane. This swing to the right I use to start my drift. If I now immediately turn left again into my curve in which I would like to drift, then pushes the vehicle rear by the mass inertia to the curve outer edge. Now I give a lot of gas or use the "clutch-kick" (as described in point 1) to move the tires to spin and initiate the drift. Again, I can now hold the vehicle in drift by means of targeted countersteering and throttle. To stop, simply interrupt the transmission of the force, go from the gas or press the clutch.

Step by step

1st speed ~ 40-50Km / h, second gear engaged
2. Before the curve: Drive to the inside of the curve
3. Then drive to the curve outside
4. immediately turn into the curve
5. Combine with full throttle, clutch kick or handbrake
6. Deflecting the drift by means of targeted gasses.

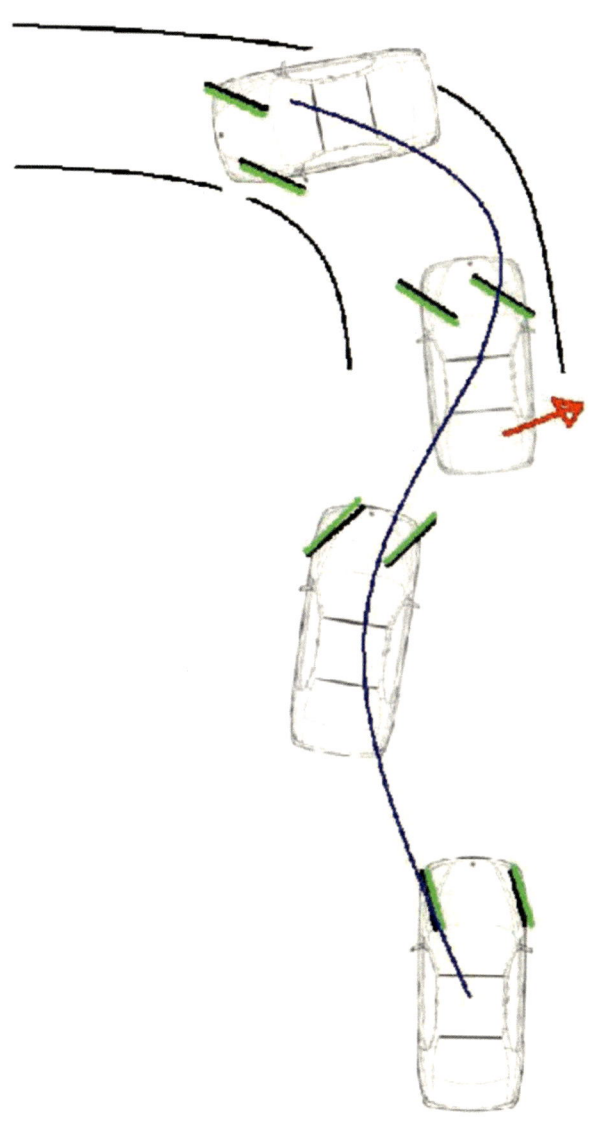

On the **red arrow** the rear swings outwards.
The **blue line** represents the driving line.

Exercise:

1. Set up a straight-forward slalom tour to find out how your vehicle behaves when it is steered. Drive this a few times.
2. Set up 3 Pylons in a row. The first two straight, the third slightly further outside. Now go through the first two pylons in the slalom, in the third you have to push the curve further and steer stronger. In this exercise, you can translate one thing to another.

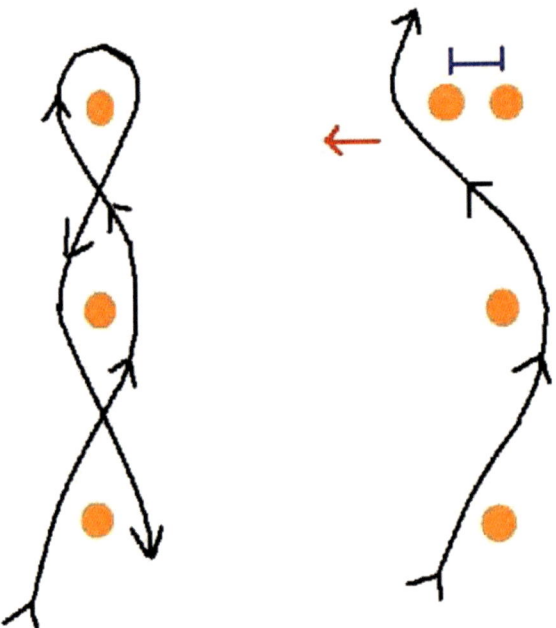

Left: A simple slalom tour that you can take off to get to know the curves of your vehicle.

Right: The top pylons were shifted slightly to the left. So you have to steer between pylons 2 and 3 more strongly to drive the curve. While you pass Pylone 3, you will notice that your vehicle is pushing some directional edge by its weight. This moment you can use to bring the vehicle together with full throttle or a clutch kick.

4. Drifting by breaking (hard)

Yes you read correctly, one can drift also by the targeted use of the brake. For this I need a slightly higher speed. When I'm in the corner, I give a short but strong brake. Due to the deceleration, the vehicle springs in front and there is a center of gravity shift to the front of the vehicle. At this moment the tail is light and breaks out. Now the moment has come again when you push the accelerator pedal to turn the wheels. This is because most vehicles have a 70% brake front and 30% rear, thus delaying your tires in the front more and it comes to a kind of Pull. This pulls back the front part of the vehicle. I have marked this as difficult, because it takes some practice, until you know how the vehicle behaves in lateral position with a full braking. Most of the time you use a combination of the rocking or I use for my part this technique, when I drive on an event on a tight curve in the drift. So I can deliberately delay the vehicle without the drift settling down and so seen in the drift into the curve brakes.

Step by step

1. Speed 50+ Km / h, second gear engaged
2. During cornering: briefly a steering pulse to the outside.
3. Immediately follow the curve and give the brake pulse.
4. The rear is light and pushes outwards.
5. Combine with full throttle or clutch kick.
6. Countersteering, holding the drift with targeted throttle

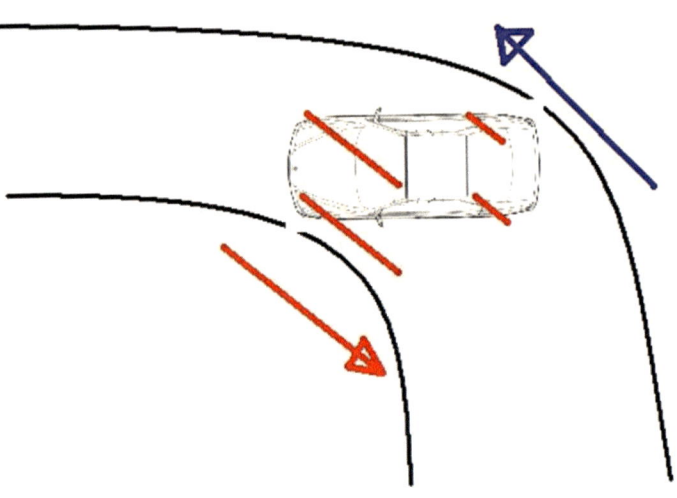

The **blue arrow** marks the **vehicle mass,** which pushes in the direction of the curve.

The **red arrow** indicates the **braking effect**. We see here that the braking force is much stronger at the front, which means that the vehicle turns.

Exercise:

1. Drive 50 km / h and make a full braking. Steer the steering wheel back and forth during the braking process to get a feel for the dynamics of your car during a braking process.
2. Drive in a large circle. You can drive as fast, until you realize that your tires are starting to squeal or start slipping. This boundary region is excellently suitable for applying the above-mentioned technique.

Note: The lighter the vehicle is at the rear, the better this technique works.

The Counter

The Counter is nothing else than the reversal in the opposite drift direction. So from left to right and from right to left. This is especially important when you are drifting on a track where you have to change the drift direction more frequently. The most important thing here is the apex, where you change the direction within a very short time. This is why the rear wheels do not have any liability. Assuming you are in a drift to the right, so you turn with your steering wheel to the left to keep the drift. If you want to change the direction, then you go a little bit from the gas. At this moment, the stern will break a little less and the drift angle will be smaller. The rear of the vehicle is positioned behind you again. You can take advantage of this situation and move the vehicle tail to your left with a strong steering pulse to the left and an additional gas pulse. Note, however, that the wheels always have to turn through, only in this way is a conversion "like on ice" possible. When you have put your vehicle rear on the right side, turn the steering wheel to the right to counter-deflect and hold the drift with controlled gas. This technique is also used to navigate on straight lines. It is also known as "Monji".

How to stop a Drift

What do I mean by that? Now and then it can happen that your vehicle breaks too much and you can not intercept the vehicle with your standard steering angle. So: your vehicle is turning more than you can compensate by counter-steering. In this case, you must make sure that the tail of your car pulls back to the lane. This is best done by making sure that the rear wheels get a bit more grip. Move away from the throttle, so the engine brake slowly decelerates the tires and minimizes lateral slippage. In addition, there is the possibility to press the clutch and thus interrupt the force supply to the rear axle. Most people will reflex the brake completely in this situation. In this case, however, it will look similar to drifting by breaking (point 4) and your vehicle will very probably turn to complete loss of control.

The Big Final

I hope you liked this workshop on Drifting and you could gain some information for you. The Driftsport is very important to me and maybe there will soon even be a new technique, which I will present on my Driftblog. I always wish you a good trip and a lot of success in trying out the above mentioned techniques. Possibly we will even see each other on the street with my promotional vehicle or an event;)

Best regards,

Simon Tillisch

Thank you very much for your Support

Dunja Nagel

Arthur „Lele" Lelonek

Michael „Gsus" Schmid

and Fiona "Fifi" Watzke

Special Thanks to Philipp Swoboda for the Translation

Important Contacts

Online Drift Academy

On my online blog I have put together a lot of useful information and also small reviews about vehicle components.

Stay in touch, visit my Website and follow me on Facebook !

→ Website : **Drift-Anleitung.de**

→ Facebook: **Online Drift Academy**

→ Get into my Facebook Group and stay in touch with other people who just started drifting or want to start !

> **Online Drift Community**

Drifting Lele

Arthur Lelonek, also known as "Drifting Lele", has helped me in the preparation of this workshop. Due to his long-term drift experience and his technical skill everyone can learn a few tricks from him. He can be reached via the Facebook-Fanpage "Drifting Lele" https://www.facebook.com/DriftingLele/

Alexander Gräff

Alex Gräff is one of the most known drifter from Germany. He´s organizing and planning events by himself and I also already participated in them. You will see him on big Events in Germany and also in different countries nearby. Stay in touch and follow him via Facebook.

→ **Alex Gräff**

Made in the USA
Monee, IL
23 July 2025

21773386R00021